Funding Your Vision

New Hope for Non-Profits

By:
Gerald H. Twombly, President
Development Marketing
Associates, Inc.

Phone toll-free: 1-866-DMA-FIRST

http://www.developmentmarketing.com

Printed in U.S.A. by
Evangel Press
Nappanee, Indiana 46550

TO SUE

*With whom I have learned and experienced what
it means to live in a relationship.*

Table of Contents

Prologue

It's hard to live with potential.

Whether you're an entrepreneur, a salesman, a provider of services, or the president of your own company; it's difficult to know that you have something that others need and they don't know it. Or, don't even seem to care.

Sometimes you want people to buy. And sometimes you want them to give. But what you really want is for them to understand your mission and to support it.

It's hard to struggle along when you really don't need to.

An Introduction

Once there was a very Frustrated Man.

The man was very gifted. He was also very consumed. He had committed himself to a great task.

The man had a vision for what he wanted to accomplish in conjunction with his work. He could see the results of what he wanted to do but could not see the means to achieve the desired results. He worked very hard to reach his goals but often felt that he was treading water, expending a lot of energy but not making much forward progress.

The man needed to raise money for his work. He needed to engage volunteers to assist him in the work. The man needed to communicate to others the nature of the enterprise. But some people didn't even know about his work and many of those who did, didn't really seem to care.

He was a very Frustrated Man.

Chapter One: The Meeting

One day The Frustrated Man was sharing his concerns with a friend.

"You know," he said, "the work we are doing is very important. In fact, if we only had the money, we could accomplish so much to improve our city. The work we are doing is also essential to the well-being of many people in our community. Everyone benefits either directly or indirectly from what we do."

"I know of your work," the friend responded, "and I believe you are right. My own family has benefitted very much from what you do and so, in fact, have many other people I know. I think your work is one of our communities best kept secrets!"

"That's just the problem," the Frustrated Man continued, "many people seem to appreciate what we do, but few lend a hand to help us continue our important work."

"What you need to do is to tell others about your work. If people only knew, they probably would want to help you. If a lot of people came alongside and shared

---

"What you need to do is tell others about your work.
If people only knew, they probably would want to help you."

---

your load, think of how much more you could accomplish."

"Maybe you're right, but that's easier said than done,"

commented the Frustrated Man. "Whenever we try something, no one seems to listen. And if they do listen, they really don't seem to care."

The friend of the Frustrated Man listened attentively as he shared his concerns. There are so many worthy causes that are committed to helping others improve themselves. Each year he had read of many that had closed their doors and others who had to restrict their outreach severely because others didn't seem to care. As he listened he was reminded of a man that others had called the Visionary, a man who had helped hundreds of organizations like the one represented by the Frustrated Man. He had helped these organizations help themselves and, in so doing, had helped multiplied thousands.

"You know," the friend said, "several months ago I was talking with another man who was once very frustrated. He was involved in a very worthy work, much like your own. He shared with me a similar story but told me of someone who had helped him to achieve his goals."

"Oh really?" said the Frustrated Man. "I have heard about all kinds of help that is supposed to be available for people like me, but I have never received much assistance from them."

"Well, I hear this man is different," he continued, "He is called the Visionary."

"That's a strange name," the Frustrated Man pondered. "Why do you think they call him that?"

"I understand he helps people achieve their vision for their work. He seems to know how to engage the support of others." As the friend spoke, he absently seemed to search his pockets, "Oh here," he said, "I thought I had one. Here is one of his business cards. It might be worth giving him a call."

For several weeks the Frustrated Man walked around

with the card of the Visionary in his jacket pocket. One day he looked at the card and read the words, "helping others to achieve their vision." He was intrigued by the claim and, at the same time, suspicious. He wondered if anyone could really help him.

"I suppose," he thought aloud, "it can't hurt to give him a call. Maybe he can share with me something that could help. I'm sure my work is worth the risk." He dialed the number, apprehensive at what he might hear when the phone stopped ringing.

"Hello." The voice seemed almost cheerful at the other end. "This is the office of the Visionary. May I help you?"

"Why yes," he stammered. "I'm involved in a very worthy work and, well, I seem to have some problems. Really, I'm not sure what I need. You see, I'm kind of confused, even. . . "

". . . even a bit frustrated?" she asked.

"I suppose that would describe it," the Frustrated Man responded. "Someone gave me the card of the Visionary a few weeks ago, and, well, I was wondering if there might be a chance to meet him and share with him my needs."

"Oh yes," the receptionist responded enthusiastically. "That's exactly what the Visionary loves to do. Let me see," she paused, "I think he could see you Tuesday morning at ten, would that be possible for you?"

"Yes, that would be fine," said the Frustrated Man. "But he doesn't even know who I am and what I do. Do you think he would really want to take the time to talk with me?"

"I know he would," the receptionist said confidently. "You see, the Visionary likes to share with others who are frustrated. You see, he too was once a very Frustrated Man."

Chapter Two: The Need for Relationships

On Tuesday the Frustrated Man made his way to the office of the Visionary.

When he arrived he was greeted warmly by the receptionist. She acted as kind in person as she had on the telephone. She poured him a cup of coffee and encouraged him to sit in the reception area until the time of his appointment.

Exactly at ten that morning the Visionary walked out of his office. "Welcome," he said warmly, "I am so glad that you have come today. Won't you come in?"

The Frustrated Man was taken back by the warmth of his reception. Together they walked into the office. The room was quite large. Against one wall was a large oak roll-top desk and on the opposite wall a brick fireplace. Hardwood floors added a feeling of warmth to the room. It was almost homey. A braided rug lay in front of the burning fireplace. The Visionary directed the Frustrated Man to one of the two large overstuffed chairs in front of the fireplace as he sat in the other.

"Well, I understand that you are frustrated?" he began.

The Frustrated Man was surprised that the Visionary so quickly seemed to get to the point. Uneasily he responded, "Uh, yes. I'm involved in a very worthy work, you see, and it seems that we are never quite able to achieve our goals. We help many people but we constantly struggle to keep going, and it's as if nobody really cares much about what we do, to say nothing about whether we continue to exist."

"That certainly is justification for a little frustration,

I'd think," smiled the Visionary. "And if there is any comfort," he continued, "I know many people in your shoes who feel the same way. In fact, there was a time when I worked with an organization, like yours, and I was very frustrated too."

"Your receptionist told me that," the Frustrated Man responded. "What happened with you? How did you overcome your frustration?"

"I learned, like most people," the Visionary said, "through a long string of mistakes. I was determined to understand why people didn't support my work because it was very worthy of support."

"And what did you learn?" the Frustrated Man asked expectantly.

"I learned that the long term success of any worthy work is directly proportional to how successfully those involved in that work build relationships with others," said the Visionary.

"Relationships?" the Frustrated Man responded sounding confused. "My organization has helped hundreds of people, and hundreds of others have participated in things we have done. I know and have spoken to

---

". . . the long term success of any worthy work is directly proportional to how successfully those involved in the work build relationships with others."

---

thousands. If there is anything we have done, it is build relationships."

"Oh," the Visionary continued, "that was true of me as well. But I later learned that there are different kinds of relationships."

"I'm not sure I understand," the Frustrated Man said.

"Well, let me put it this way," the Visionary responded. "If you are to be successful in the work to which you have committed yourself, it is essential that you sustain the involvement of others."

The Frustrated Man nodded. Part of his frustration was the result of always scrambling to garner the support to continue the work. He would be involved in a variety of activities, would work hard to solicit the support of people in a variety of ways only to have to repeat the process again and again.

The Visionary continued to speak. "The relationships you develop will be one of two kinds. Some of them will be emotional. People will hear about your work, be moved emotionally by what you do, and will often choose to support you in ways convenient to them. There will be other people who will clearly understand the mission to which you have committed yourself and will

---

" . . . only the support you receive from those with whom you have a rational relationship is sustainable."

---

choose to support you because of their understanding of that mission. I categorize this second group as those with rational relationships. The thing you must always remember is that only the support you receive from those with whom you have rational relationships is sustainable."

"What happens with emotional relationships?" the Frustrated Man asked. "I receive a lot of support each year from people who fall into that category."

"Oh yes, I know," responded the Visionary. "But because they support you for emotional reasons, the only way they will continue their involvement with you is if you repeat the emotional experience that prompted their involvement in the first place."

The Frustrated Man thought about that statement. So often he had felt like he was treading water in his work. He was expending energy just to stay afloat and when he was finished, he was quick to realize that he had made little forward progress. It seemed that he was always trying to complete a never-ending list of activities and projects. He was exhausted but, much worse, so were most of the volunteers who assisted him.

"I think I understand," the Frustrated Man said. "The support I receive from people with whom I have only an emotional relationship is not really sustainable?"

"Exactly," said the Visionary. "The only way you can sustain emotional support is to repeat the emotion. And that can become very exhausting."

"The good news is there is a better way. There is a way that you can gain support for your work that will sustain itself year after year."

"Boy, can I relate to that!" the Frustrated Man sighed.

"The good news is," the Visionary brightened, "that there is a better way. There is a way that you can gain support for your work that will sustain itself year after year. You know," he added, "too many who work in organizations like yours work very hard. It's as if they are building a house. They work diligently day after day for an entire year to build this beautiful house. But on the last day of the year they take a bulldozer and plow the house down. Wouldn't it be better if, rather than building the house and tearing it down year after year, they spent one year pouring the footers, another year building the foundation, and subsequent years, adding to the structure in a pre-planned manner? Imagine, after a few years they would have a very beautiful house with the infrastructure in place to help it last for many years to come."

"Makes sense to me," the Frustrated Man added.

"Well, that is the better way," the Visionary continued. "And through my struggles and mistakes, that is what I discovered."

"Can you teach me how?" the Frustrated Man asked hopefully.

"Absolutely. But we must take it one step at a time. Why don't you come back next week and we'll begin our journey together."

Chapter Three: Identifying Your Prospects

W hen the Frustrated Man arrived the next week at the office of the Visionary, he already had experienced some personal relief. The earlier session had caused him to analyze certain aspects of his work. He realized that many of the relationships he had were, in fact, emotional in their orientation. When he assessed the support his organization was receiving, since most of it was coming from people with whom he had only an emotional relationship, he determined that most of the support they were providing was not sustainable.

As he walked into the office of the Visionary, he felt determined. For the first time he sensed there might be hope for his organization. More importantly, he also felt that perhaps there was hope for himself.

"Today," the Visionary began, "I want to talk to you about the first step in the process of building relationships."

"And what would that be?" the Frustrated Man asked.

"The first step is to identify those people with whom you *could* build a relationship. Every organization has a very large number of potential prospects. In fact, your organization undoubtedly has all the potential prospects it would ever require to achieve your vision, no matter how large that vision might be."

"I find that a little hard to believe," the Frustrated Man observed. "You don't know how big my vision is or how much it will cost."

"It really makes no difference," the Visionary said, "all

the prospects you require are there."

"Really now," the Frustrated Man asked, "where are they?"

The Visionary answered, "There are a couple of terms

"The first step is to identify those people with whom you could build a relationship."

---

we use in marketing. The first of these is **universe**. It looks something like this."

The Visionary reached down and picked up a pad of paper. On the paper he drew a stick man and drew a small circle around him.

He continued to speak, "Let the stick man represent you and let the circle represent your sphere of influence. Every person you will ever meet is surrounded by a group of people with whom he has influence. If that person has a viewpoint, regardless of whether or not those within his sphere of influence agree with it, he has earned the right to be heard among those in his circle."

"You mean," the Frustrated Man added, "people like my wife and friends?"

"Exactly," said the Visionary. "Our sphere of influence will include our spouse, our siblings, our children, those with whom we work or go to church, personal friends, and a host of others. In fact the universe of the average person in our country is 40."

"Is that all?" the Frustrated Man asked. "I can think of many more than that personally. I would bet my sphere of influence is two or three hundred."

"It probably is," added the Visionary. "You see the size of a person's universe is determined by the roles he has played in life. A very public person, like you have always been, is likely to have a universe much larger than, say, a factory worker. But the average, nonetheless, is about 40."

The Visionary continued, "There is another term we use in marketing called *market universe*. If you were to try to draw it, it might look something like this."

He reached down again to pick up the paper tablet. On the tablet he drew a building and around the building he drew a much larger circle.

"Let's let this building represent your organization. Inside the circle we have many groups of people who are impacted by your work. There are all kinds of groups from workers, recipients of the services you provide, volunteers, community agencies, even the vendors with whom you do business. All of these groups benefit either directly or indirectly from the work that you do."

"That's a pretty large group," added the Frustrated Man. "Our work impacts people in our community who don't even know we exist!"

"That's true," agreed the Visionary. "And it is important to remember that each of these groups of people has many people within them. In other words there are lots of workers, lots of recipients of your services, lots of volunteers, and so on. In fact, market universe defined is 'the sum total of the individual universes of everyone who is impacted by your work, either directly or indirectly.' The number of people in your market universe is gigantic. It is also calculable."

"You mean," the Frustrated Man asked, "these people represent potential individuals with whom I might develop a relationship?"

"Absolutely," answered the Visionary. "You see, your organization certainly doesn't lack the potential prospects to do anything that you have ever dreamed!"

"I can see that," the Frustrated Man said, almost thinking aloud. "But it's one thing to say that there is all this potential, but quite another to do something about it."

"You're right," the Visionary agreed. "In fact, just knowing that your organization has a large market universe doesn't really mean a thing. You see, a prospect is not a legitimate prospect to your organization until you have his or her name and address permanently recorded somewhere."

" . . . your organization . . . doesn't lack the potential prospects to do anything that you have ever dreamed."

"Somewhere?" the Frustrated Man asked. "Do you mean that I need to have a bunch of cards with names and addresses on them for reference purposes?"

"Well, cards could work," the Visionary smiled, "but you will probably want to move to something a bit more sophisticated. Most organizations your size maintain a computerized database which lists the names of all their prospects. Computerization has made a lot of what we need to do much easier."

"That sounds like quite a task to me," the Frustrated Man said. "How in the world would I ever get all of those names?"

"Well there are many ways," the Visionary responded. "You already know most of the names and addresses of people who are directly associated with you. Those names are easy to get. It's some of the more distantly removed names that are harder. Perhaps we could look at how to deal with that problem during another visit."

"It sounds like we're done for today," the Frustrated Man smiled.

"I think so," the Visionary agreed. "Let's not take too much all at once. But I would like you to do something."

"Oh really? What?" asked the Frustrated Man.

"I'd like you to make a list of all the groups of people that your work impacts. Think of as many as you can, groups of people from those who benefit directly from what you do to those very remote groups who may not even know you exist."

"I can do that," the Frustrated Man answered. "But, that will be some list."

"I hope so," the Visionary smiled. "That only means we have much more potential than we may have thought at first.

Take Ten . . .

Take just ten minutes to complete the following exercises:

1. Critical Groups. Make a list of those groups of people you feel are critical to the success of your organization.

2. Impacted Groups. Develop a list of all the groups of people who are impacted either directly or indirectly by the work of your organization.

Chapter Four: Qualifying Your Prospects

Whi the Frustrated Man arrived at the office of the Visionary the next week, they immediately went to work.

"Did you complete your homework?" the Visionary asked.

"Oh yes," responded the Frustrated Man. He reached into his vest pocket and handed the Visionary a folded sheet of paper. On the paper the Frustrated Man had listed the names of fifteen specific groups of individuals. Each of the groups listed had been impacted in one way or another by the work in which he was involved.

The Visionary glanced through the list. He looked up and said, "I see that you have quite a list here. And when

---

"The second step in the process is to qualify your prospects."

---

you think of all the specific individuals who are represented in each of these groups, you've got quite a list of prospects."

"I suppose so," the Frustrated Man responded. "I'm not sure where I go from here. It's one thing to have a lot of prospects and quite another to garner their support for the things that we must do."

"You're right on that count," the Visionary smiled. "So let's see if we can continue the process we began last week. The first step in the process of building relationships is identifying those people with whom we want to build relationships. The second step in the process is to qualify your prospects."

The Visionary reached down on the table in front of him to pick up a yellow legal pad. He reached into his shirt pocket for a pen. "All the prospects you have," he began, "will fall into one of three broad categories. First, you have those who are directly benefitting from the services you provide. Since they are the most closely related to you, we will call them nuclear." The Visionary paused to write the word "nuclear" on the pad.

He continued, "Of the groups you have listed here, which ones would you think would fall into the nuclear category?"

The Frustrated Man glanced down at his list and began to enumerate them, "Well, I suppose that our clients would go on that list and certainly our staff." He paused for a moment as he glanced through the list. "I've listed our board members. I guess you could say they are pretty close to our organization."

"All of your prospects will fall into one of three broad groups."

"I'd agree with that," the Visionary said. "You might also want to add past clients to that list for they, too, have benefitted from the services you provide."

The Visionary wrote the word "Affinity" on the pad. "There is another group of your prospects who benefit indirectly from the services you provide. We call them 'affinity' prospects. They may not be directly involved, but they still benefit from the existence of your organization."

"You mean," the Frustrated Man interrupted, "people

like the family members of our clients?"

"Exactly," the Visionary agreed. "You see, the family members of clients you serve may never experience your work first hand, but to the extent that your clients have benefitted from what you do, they indirectly benefit as well. Can you think of other groups?"

The Frustrated Man looked through the list. "I suppose our vendors would fall into that category and maybe even the employers of those clients we serve."

"Okay, you're on the right track now." The Visionary wrote the word "Fringe" on the pad in front of him. "We call the third broad group of prospects fringe. This group has a geographic association with your work. They may not even know that you exist! But regardless of that, these groups work, live, and function in the same region where you provide your services."

"Would that include many of the businesses and corporations in our community?" the Frustrated Man asked.

"Yes," agreed the Visionary. "You might also include influential political leaders in your community, service clubs, and some charitable foundations, too."

The Frustrated Man was looking at his list and writing letters after each group he had identified. "I understand what you are saying," he said, "but I'm not sure I understand the significance of it."

The Visionary looked as if he was going to say something very significant. "There is an important rule you must remember when building your organization. This rule is foundational to all that you will be doing. It's called the rule of linkage. The rule of linkage defined simply is this: the closer someone is linked to you, the more likely they will be to support you."

"Oh, I see," the Frustrated Man's eyes brightened. "These groups that fall under the category 'nuclear' are more likely to support my work than those that fall into the 'fringe' category."

"Exactly," agreed the Visionary. "It's also important to remember that there are two kinds of linkage. You have what I call 'natural' linkage and you can also have 'created' linkage."

"I understand the words," the Frustrated Man said, "but I'm not sure I understand how it relates to all we are talking about."

There is one rule that is foundational
to all that you do.
It's called the rule of linkage.

The Visionary nodded and said, "I am the youngest in my family. I have two older sisters. I'm sure there were times when my sisters might have wanted to disown me, but the reality is that I could point to my parents, as they could, and remind my sisters that they were my parents too. But imagine," he continued, "that my parents adopted a child into the family. Despite the fact that that child was not biologically linked with my sisters and me, he or she would be an equal member of the family by virtue of the adoptive process."

The Frustrated Man brightened. "I understand," he said. "There was 'natural' linkage between you and your sisters and 'created' linkage between you and the adopted child."

"Exactly," said the Visionary. "And one of the most important things you will have to remember as you begin to build a program for your work is that it will be very advantageous for you to create linkage among those groups with whom you do not have it naturally. By doing so, you increase the likelihood that they will support the causes you represent."

"But, how do you do that?" the Frustrated Man asked. "How do you create linkage?"

"One of the most important things you will have to remember ... is that it will be very advantageous for you to create linkage among those groups with whom you do not have it naturally."

"Oh, there are many ways," the Visionary said. "If I asked one of my affinity prospects to serve on a committee, I have created linkage. If I began a 'Corporate Advisory Counsel,' I would be creating linkage between some of my fringe prospects and my organization. Whenever you recruit a volunteer to assist you, you create linkage."

"I'm beginning to understand all of this," the Frustrated Man said. "The more I do things to create linkage among people with whom I do not have it naturally, the more likely people will tend to support my work. Is that right?"

"Absolutely!" the Visionary agreed. "Whenever you categorize a prospect by the closeness of his association with you, you have qualified him. But there are other ways in which you might qualify prospects. If you have someone with whom you are working that has a professional skill, say an architect, and you are about to add on to your building, you might want to recruit him to assist you with the drawings."

"I see," the Frustrated Man said enthusiastically. "I could qualify people on the basis of occupation?"

"That's right," the Visionary agreed. "You can qualify

people on the basis of their need for your services or whether or not they might be a good volunteer. There are many ways."

The Frustrated Man smiled. "It kind of reminds me of my dating days, before I was married. When I was young, I thought the world was the field. I was single and so were thousands of eligible girls. I had identified the prospects!" He continued, "But when you get right down to it, I did have some qualifications. I wanted a girl that I was physically attracted to, one that shared my interests, and one that I could enjoy as a friend for the rest of my life. I guess I qualified the prospects, didn't I?"

The Visionary agreed. "You sure did. And it's interesting to me how much like courtship the process of building relationships between our organizations and its prospects really is. In fact, next week let's look at the next step in the process, cultivation, in terms of courtship!"

Take Ten . . .

Take just ten minutes to complete the following:

1. Categorize by Linkage. Take the lists from the previous exercise and categorize each group on the basis of their linkage with you (nuclear, affinity, or fringe).

2. Categorize in Other Ways. Think of other ways in which you might qualify a group. List several areas where you may have needs, *e.g.* donors, volunteers, clients, etc. and under each heading, list those groups that could assist you.

Chapter Five: The Role of Emotion in Relationships

The image of courtship captured the imagination of the Frustrated Man during the week. He fondly remembered the days in which he dated his spouse, the places they had gone and the things they had shared together. They spent a great deal of time talking during those days, learning about the interests they had in common and the things that concerned them. It seemed they spent a lot of time talking.

The relationship the Frustrated Man enjoyed with his spouse was very special. Oh, they had their disagreements and occasionally they would simply agree to disagree. But there was a core commitment to each other that was the solid foundation upon which they grew in their relationship with one another. They had learned to give as well as to receive from one another. In thinking about how to define relationships, the Frustrated Man couldn't think of anything other than the relationship in life that he enjoyed the most.

But now the Visionary was talking about building relationships on another level. The Frustrated Man felt competent in building relationships individually but didn't have any idea about how that could be done in conjunction with his work. He was quite sincere in wanting to establish relationships and wanted to talk to the Visionary about the difference between simply manipulating people to do what you want them to do and building a true relationship.

He arrived at the office of the Visionary with all kinds

of questions and was glad when he was invited to share some of his concerns.

"I have learned much from our time together already," the Frustrated Man began. "But what I fear is that we may be building relationships for selfish purposes and simply developing a scheme to get people to do what we want. I guess I don't want to do that, it sounds too much like manipulation to me."

"If the only reason you pursue a relationship is for what you can gain from it, that is manipulation."

The Visionary nodded. In over twenty-five years of helping others to achieve their vision, this was the one question that was raised the most.

"That's a very legitimate concern," he began. "People obviously don't feel good about being used. And that's why I call what it is we are doing a relationship-building model. There is a lot to be gained from relationships. Both parties benefit from a good relationship. There is giving and there is receiving. And you must never forget that. If the only reason you pursue a relationship is for what you can gain from it, then that is manipulation. But if you pursue relationships for the right reasons, it is mutually rewarding and will be for many, many years."

"That's what I want," the Frustrated Man continued. "You know, this week I couldn't escape the idea you introduced last week. The idea of courtship. Well, I began to think about the relationship I enjoy with my wife. And well, this might sound a little strange, but if I could build relationships with others like the one I enjoy with her . . . " The Frustrated Man was having difficulty expressing his desire.

"I understand thoroughly," the Visionary broke in. "And that's where we are going. You remember the very first time we met and I talked to you about sustainable relationships?"

"Yes," the Frustrated Man answered.

"Well, *relationships are sustainable only when they are rooted in a commitment to someone or something.* Relationships often begin for emotional reasons. I imagine you were attracted to your wife for emotional reasons before you courted her." The Visionary smiled.

"You're right about that," the Frustrated Man agreed. "She was the prettiest girl in my class, a cheerleader, and everybody's ideal."

"She sounds quite lovely," the Visionary said. "But you must remember that, while emotion might have brought you together initially, you stay together for totally different reasons. It's your commitment to one another and your commitment to the relationship that keeps you together."

". . . emotion might have brought you together . . .
but it's your commitment to one another . . .
that keeps you together."

The Visionary was wanting to make a shift in their thinking. "The process of building relationships organizationally is very similar to the steps you went through in building a relationship with your wife. It's just that we are dealing with more people."

"Tracking the development of those relationships has to be pretty challenging," the Frustrated Man said. "I mean, I had enough difficulty trying to keep track of what was happening with one person. And yet, if my organization is to be successful, it will mean that I will have to build relationships with hundreds. Maybe thousands. Is that really possible?"

"Yes, it is possible, and yes, it is challenging," the Visionary agreed.

"I'm ready to learn," the Frustrated Man said enthusiastically.

"And I'm ready to show you," the Visionary said. "But what I would like to share with you now is going to take a little while. It's among the most important things I have to share with you so I hope you have a few extra minutes this week."

"I've got all the time you need," the Frustrated Man said.

"Well then, let me begin."

Take Ten . . .

Take just ten minutes to evaluate your current relationships.

1. Group Listing. List all of those groups with whom you have already had success in developing some kind of relationship.

2. Relationship Evaluation. Place a letter "E" or "R" after each listed group representing whether or not you assess that relationship to be predominantly emotional or rational.

Chapter Six: Bringing People into Your "House"

The Visionary had grown up near the sea. As a youth he had seen fishing boats arrive from weeks at sea and was intrigued as they emptied their catch at the end of the trip. In the hold of the ship were a variety of fish. There were cod and haddock, flounder, and sole. The sea yielded an abundant harvest.

This image of youth never left him. As he observed organizations that were struggling to stay alive, he had a very visual picture of their potential back in the recesses of his mind.

In attempting to relay that picture he began to speak. "I would like to imagine your organization as a beautiful house. The house sits alone on a high hill. The house has many well appointed rooms, a beautiful foyer, a large front door, and a spacious porch. The house I am asking you to imagine," he continued, "stands next to the sea."

"Sounds like a pretty inviting place," the Frustrated Man responded.

"Indeed it is," said the Visionary. "But unfortunately, most people don't know what is in the house. Many people have passed by and admired it, others have heard about the house but have never seen it, and still others don't even know this beautiful house exists in their community." In his efforts to make the analogy even more vivid he continued by saying, "The sad thing is that the people who live in this house are eager to extend hospitality to everyone."

"So why don't they just invite people in?" asked the Frustrated Man.

"Well, that's exactly the point that I want to make," commented the Visionary. "You see, if this house represents your organization, you know all about what happens inside the house. You know the differences your organization is making in the lives of people because you experience it everyday. Unfortunately, most of the people with whom you will want to build relationships have no idea what is happening inside your organization."

"Tell me more," the Frustrated Man said.

"Imagine the sea as being filled with fish," the Visionary said as his thoughts went back to the vision of his youth. "Let these fish represent the prospects that you have already identified. They are almost innumerable and they represent an answer to virtually every need you will ever have. You see," he continued, "all the money your organization will ever need is in the sea; every client you may want to serve is in the sea; all the volunteers you will ever require are in the sea and much more."

"Wow," the Frustrated Man breathed, "that is a staggering thought."

"It is indeed," the Visionary responded. "But, unfortunately having a beautiful house, having the desire to share it with others, and having a 'sea' full of prospects will never enable you to achieve your potential. Some very important things need to happen."

"It seems we have done something already," the Frustrated Man added. "We at least know that the sea is filled with legitimate prospects!"

"You're right, but now we need to talk about what must happen, what you must do to take advantage of the great potential that you have as an organization." The Visionary reached down to his pad and drew the scene he had just described on a sheet of paper. He drew a line from the sea to the front porch of the house. "The first step in achieving your potential will require that you bring people out of the sea on to the front porch. I call that the entry level opportunity."

"The first step in achieving your potential will require that you bring people out of the sea on to the front porch."

"I see that providing that opportunity is essential," said the Frustrated Man, "but isn't that a lot of work."

"Not at all," commented the Visionary. "In fact, you are already doing it. But, unfortunately, if you are like most organizations, you have left many people on the porch outside the house."

"Now, you really have me confused," said the Frustrated Man.

"Let's talk first about what you are already doing to bring people out of the sea of prospects onto your front porch," said the Visionary. "Every time someone participates in a program or a project that you sponsor, he comes out of the sea and moves to your front porch. Whenever you present a program to a group of people, you are bringing those who listen to you from the sea on to the porch of your organization."

"Unbelievable," the Frustrated Man whispered. "We often promote our organization through special programs. Do you mean to tell me that everyone who has ever participated in those programs has come out of the sea?"

"Exactly," exclaimed the Visionary. "It's important to remember that it will often be emotion that will bring someone out of the sea to the front porch of your house, but getting people to the front porch is only the beginning."

"What do you mean?" asked the Frustrated Man.

"Well, if I were driving through your neighborhood and showed up one morning on your front porch, what would you do?" asked the Visionary.

"I'd invite you in," the Frustrated Man said, looking confused.

"Exactly!" responded the Visionary enthusiastically. "And that is the next essential step you must remember. You see, your invitation for me to enter your home would require a response from me. I might tell you 'No, I really don't care to come in,' or 'I'm sorry, I'm on my way to somewhere else and really don't have time to come in,' or 'Yes, thank you, I will be pleased to come in.'"

"And why is that so significant?" asked the Frustrated Man.

"Because the moment I am asked to make a decision, I am being asked to make a *rational* decision. And, more importantly," the Visionary continued, "once I step into the foyer of your home, the relationship between us has changed. You see, it may have been emotion that brought me to your porch but it will always be rationalism that will bring me into the foyer."

". . . it may have been emotion that brought me onto your porch, but it will always be rationalism that will bring me into the foyer."

"And it is only rational support that is sustainable," the Frustrated Man said proudly.

"Right you are!" the Visionary said with satisfaction. "And the invitation you extended forces the issue. I call the invitation 'the bridge' and when someone accepts the invitation and comes into the foyer I call the results 'conversion.'"

The Frustrated Man was busily writing on a sheet of paper. He looked up and asked, "I see where you are going but I'm not sure I can understand how it plays out practically in my organization."

The Visionary nodded, seeming to understand. "That is the challenge. Can you think of some event that you sponsor each year that might bring people to your 'front porch?'"

The Frustrated Man thought for a moment and then suggested, "Well, every year we have a Christmas program that we open up to the community. Would that qualify?"

"Yes," answered the Visionary. "Now, first of all you must remember that *prospects aren't prospects until you have their names permanently recorded somewhere.* All the people who come to your Christmas program are prospects and they are good prospects. You didn't rope them and drag them in," he smiled. "They came because they chose to come."

The Visionary continued. "Your first objective should be to get the names of those who were there. If you fail to do that, you've committed a very bad mistake."

The Frustrated Man looked embarrassed. "I'm afraid I've let a lot of opportunities go by," he said sheepishly. "But, really, how do you do that?"

"There are several things you might consider," the Visionary responded. "Some organizations merely use a guest book, but probably the best way is simply to enclose a registration card in the evening's program."

"And you ask people to register their attendance?" the Frustrated Man asked.

"Yes, but there's more," continued the Visionary. "You might add a couple of boxes on the card that people could check. One might make a qualifying statement like, 'I am a client' or something similar. That could be helpful to you as you are entering names into your organization's computerized database. Many people who will be at your program will already be on your prospect list and this will help you to separate them from those who have no affiliation with you. They are the ones whom you would like to add to your list of prospects."

"I understand," the Frustrated Man commented.

"But the next boxes on your registration card are even more important." The Visionary acted like he was going to make an important point. "Say you have a box that says, 'I would like to receive your organization's free newsletter' or 'I would like to receive Organizational Updates from you.' If anyone checks one of those boxes, they have told you that they are interested in you and your work."

"It's like I have extended to them an invitation to come off the porch into the house."

"There you go," the Visionary responded approvingly. "And once they accept that invitation, the relationship has changed. Now you can take them around and show them your house."

The Frustrated Man feverishly wrote notes and observations on the sheet of paper in front of him. He was beginning to see the light and to have a new hope for his organization. His burden seemed to be lifting and he could hardly wait for their next meeting.

Take Ten . . .

Take just ten minutes to think through those things you are doing to bring people into your "house."

1. Entry Level Opportunities. Make a list of all the opportunities your organization provides to bring people out of your "sea of prospects."

2. Bridging Opportunities. Make a list of the specific efforts your organization has made to "invite" those who have responded to your entry level opportunity into your "house."

Chapter Seven: Tracking the Development of Relationships

During the week, the Frustrated Man had begun to think through the things he was already doing to share with others the needs of his organization. The previous meeting had forced him to think with a new set of terms. He began to write the letters 'E' and 'B' after events to define whether it was or could be an entry level opportunity or a bridging exercise.

It seemed that he was gathering information much more quickly than he had the ability to process it. When he arrived for their weekly meeting, the Visionary began by introducing a new idea.

"I want to talk to you today about your database," he began. "We have made some reference to it in our previous conversations, but it is important now that we begin to focus more on this essential part of what you will need to do in your organization."

"When you refer to a database, I am assuming that you are talking about how my organization chooses to maintain essential information on prospects. Is that what you mean?" the Frustrated Man asked.

"Exactly," replied the Visionary. "There are a variety of ways in which you might permanently store that data but today, given that computer technology is relatively inexpensive, I strongly recommend that you use that medium."

"What kind of software do you need?" asked the

Frustrated Man.

"There are commercial programs that are available, written especially for organizations like yours," answered the Visionary. "Many organizations just beginning to think through these kinds of issues will purchase some packaged programs at a local computer store. The best of these programs are called 'integrated' in that they include three or four program modules in one. You definitely need a program that has a database module, something that you can program to accommodate the unique needs of your organization. In addition, you will want a word processing module that can take information from your database and merge it into a document like a letter. Many of the popular programs also include a spreadsheet module."

"An integrated program allows for all the modules to work together?" asked the Frustrated Man.

"That's right," responded the Visionary, "and that can be very important to you. You can input the names and addresses of your prospects into letters, print addresses directly on to envelopes, and sort information in a variety of creative and very helpful ways."

"What kind of information would you want to store on the prospects we have identified?" asked the Frustrated Man.

The Visionary took his note pad and began to write down items as he shared them with the Frustrated Man. "First, you will need the name and address of your prospect. You should store other pertinent data like phone numbers, giving details, and other items that will enable you to track a developing relationship."

"What do you mean, items to track the developing relationship?"

The Visionary continued, "Information is stored in

what is called a field. You will have several 'fields' within any individual database record. Let's say that we have a record that looks something like this." As he spoke the Visionary wrote on his sheet:

John L. Doe

3 Maple Street

Indianapolis, IN 46589

"Now," he added, "all of this is important information. You know your prospect's name and address. But, if you had a field that had recorded within it the letter "N" you would have even more information."

"Oh really," queried the Frustrated Man, "and what would that be?"

"In this record," the Visionary responded, "the 'N' stands for Nuclear. We know that John Doe has been categorized as a nuclear prospect. He has the closest linkage to us in that he benefits directly from the services we provide. Based on that piece of information we might conclude, at least tentatively, that John Doe might be very likely to respond positively to our invitations for help."

"Well that makes sense. He has the closest linkage," the Frustrated Man responded. "But there must be more."

"Oh yes," responded the Visionary. "Let's say there is another field with the letter 'C' in it. The 'C' stands for Client. Now we know a bit more about John Doe. He is a client of the organization you represent. Now," the Visionary added, "we could write a letter to John Doe and acknowledge the relationship that we know exists between him and our organization."

The Frustrated Man was busy taking notes on a pad of

paper. He looked up, wiped his brow and said, "O.K., I'm beginning to understand. But how is this going to help me track a relationship?" he asked.

"Good question," the Visionary nodded approvingly. "Let's say there is another field, and in that field you have the letter 'D.' Let's assume that this letter represents where that particular prospect is in comparison to an ideal profile."

"An ideal profile?" the Frustrated Man asked, a look of confusion on his face.

"A profile represents a picture of the ideal relationship you would like to have with your prospects," the Visionary explained. "Some of your prospects might match your definition of the ideal perfectly so we'll call them 'A' prospects. Some may match it in many ways, so we'll call them 'B' prospects, some may match the profile in some ways, we'll call them 'C' prospects, and some may not match it at all, we'll call them 'D's'."

"So you mean," the Frustrated Man asked, "that John Doe is really not in a very close relationship with the organization, despite the fact that he is related to us in a nuclear way?"

"You're a quick learner," the Visionary replied. "And, if the facts were known, you could appeal to John Doe from now until the end of time and he would never respond affirmatively

"So what should happen?" asked the Frustrated Man.

"Your goal with John Doe should be to bring him from where he is, a 'D' categorized prospect to a 'C' categorized prospect," the Visionary responded.

"Well, I guess the next question is how?" smiled the Frustrated Man.

"You are asking the right question, all right," agreed the Visionary, "but I want to reserve that for a little later.

Let me say now," he continued, "that at some point in time you should know where every single person on your database is in relationship to your organization."

" . . . you should know where every single person on your database is in relationship to your organization."

"You mean," the Frustrated Man repeated with some astonishment, "that I should know where *every* person on my database is in relationship to my organization? My word," he gasped, "that means I'll need information on literally thousands of people."

"Pretty challenging, right?" smiled the Visionary.

"To say the least," he responded.

"Well it is possible, and it is not that difficult. But before we talk about the process, think about the potential. Imagine what a difference it would be for you to know who all of your 'A' categorized prospects were. And then, if you only knew who your 'D' categorized prospects were, you might be able to do something about it!"

"I can think of all kinds of things I could do," the Frustrated Man agreed, "and it might save me a great deal of money. It probably doesn't make sense to treat all prospects alike, especially when it is pretty certain that some won't ever respond."

"You *are* catching on," laughed the Visionary.

"O.K.," smiled the Frustrated Man, "I think I understand what you mean about tracking but I'm still dying to know how I do it. After all, I do have a rather limited number of people to assist me."

"Let's make that the focus of our next visit, all right?"
"That's fine with me."

Take Ten . . .

Take just ten minutes to evaluate your database.

1. Fields. What fields would your organization require in order to track the development of emerging relationships effectively?

2. Preliminary Evaluation. What percentage of your current database would you estimate as being categorized as A, B, C, or D?

Chapter Eight: The Secret of Cultivation

During the intervening week the Frustrated Man had begun to think what he would do if he knew where various prospects were in relationship to his organization. He had lots of ideas about what he could do and was even beginning to see that it really could be done. The Visionary had expanded his vision and for the first time, he really could see that his own vision for the great work in which he was involved was achievable.

The Visionary had made everything sound rather simple. The Frustrated Man was still uncertain, however, how all the things that he had been told were important to do could be done. He walked into the office of the Visionary with many questions.

"I hope," he began, "that we can continue where we left off last week." He went on to explain, "I really understand the value of knowing where people are in relationship to you but I am still finding it hard to figure out how that is possible, given the large number of prospects we have to deal with."

"I thought the same way for many years," the Visionary responded. "One day a colleague of mine came up with a very helpful acronym and since the day he shared it with me, it has been the basis of my instruction to others on this very important point."

"An acronym?" the Frustrated Man asked, "is that when each letter of the word is the first letter of another word?"

"Yes," nodded The Visionary. "The acronym that was shared with me was the word AID. Each letter represents something. The 'A' stands for the word 'attendance,' the letter 'I' for 'involvement,' and the letter 'D' for 'donation.' If you use this guide to evaluate your prospects in relation to your organization, you'll get a pretty clear picture of where people are."

"I don't understand," the Frustrated Man responded.

"Think of it this way," the Visionary continued, "if one of your prospects has attended one of your organization's activities, has been involved in some way in something you have done, and has made a contribution of either his time or resources, let's call him a category 'A' prospect. If he has done two of the three, let's call him a 'B' prospect, if he has done one of the three things, let's refer to him as a 'C' prospect, and if he has done none of the three, lets call him a 'D'."

"Oh, I see," said the Frustrated Man. "The John Doe that we looked at last week had never attended anything we had sponsored, had never been actively involved in anything beyond his client relationship with us, and had never given anything to us. I'm beginning to catch on."

"Yes, you are," the Visionary said proudly. "And the goal for John Doe is to move him from a category 'D' to a 'C' prospect. If we are successful in doing that, we have increased the likelihood of his sustained involvement in our work." The Visionary asked, "Can you conceive of some ways you might be able to change the relational status of John Doe with you?"

"Well," he stammered, "I suppose if he came to something we did, that would make him a 'C' prospect, wouldn't it?"

The Visionary smiled triumphantly, "Yes, it would. But if you could then secure his involvement in something, as a volunteer or committee person, you would raise him from a C to a B."

"This is all rather staggering," said the Frustrated Man. "Instead of one relationship-building program, I might have three or four going on at the same time."

"That's right, and probably even more than that," agreed the Visionary. "You might have a program designed to bring fringe 'D' prospects to 'C' prospects, another to bring Affinity 'D' prospects to 'C' prospects, etc. But rather than think about the work, think about the results. Mass mailings to even semi-qualified prospects might yield a 3% response. But a special request to a group of Category 'A' cultivated prospects might yield a 50% response. Sometimes, even more."

"A special request to a group of 'A' categorized and cultivated prospects might yield a 50% response!"

"If we would get a 3% response, our board would be euphoric," laughed the Frustrated Man. "If they ever got a 50% response, we'd have to bring in the heart machines!"

The two laughed. There was a special bonding process taking place between the Frustrated Man and the Visionary. They seemed to understand one another, and the Frustrated Man felt safe when he was with the Visionary. Rather than being lectured to, he was being mentored. He really liked the feeling.

"That's the difference good cultivation strategies can make," the Visionary said. "When you asked your spouse to marry you, my guess is you were pretty assured that she would say 'yes' weren't you?"

"You bet I was," the Frustrated Man smiled. "You don't think I invested in all those meals and spent all those hours sharing my heart with her for nothing do you?"

"Of course you didn't," agreed the Visionary. "But think of your work in the same way. When cultivation has been successful, solicitation will be successful. In the course of my career I have asked hundreds of people to invest in a variety of ways in the organizations I represented. Do you know something? I think I can count on the fingers of one hand the times I have been turned down."

"When cultivation has been successful, solicitation will be successful."

"Really?" The Frustrated Man looked amazed.

"Really," he affirmed. "And the reason is not that I am so persuasive; it's because I completed my homework and never asked anyone until I knew they were ready. By the time I came to them they *rationally* understood the mission to which my organization was committed and had moved into *relationship* with that organization."

"Something like picking apples in an orchard at harvest time," said the Frustrated Man.

"Exactly," agreed the Visionary. "And that's the way it should be."

Take Ten . . .

Take just ten minutes to discover what you might do to enhance your relationships with others.

1. Attendance. What kinds of activities could we freely invite people to attend?

2. Involvement. In what ways can people become involved in our organization?

3. Donation. How can people contribute to our organization?

Chapter Nine: Turning Activities into Events

The Frustrated Man had taken on a new outlook in relation to his organization. His weeks under the tutelage of the Visionary had given him a grasp of the task at hand. He realized that building relationships was important, but what was more important was the quality of those relationships.

As they had walked out of the office at their last meeting the Visionary had said something that had stuck in his mind. "You know, my friend, you are already doing many of the things you should be doing to be effective in building relationships. What you need to do now is to take advantage of all those things."

The Frustrated Man had thought all week of the things he did. He began to glance through his calendar and the calendar of his organization. There were all kinds of events planned, events that he felt could probably be used to help him achieve his new goals.

As he walked into the office of the Visionary he looked at him and smiled, "Well, you did it again."

"What's that?" the Visionary asked, looking surprised.

"As I left last week you said that I was already doing many of the things I need to be doing to accomplish my relationship-building goals," he explained. "But you kind of left me to hold the thought and I haven't gotten much rest all week trying to figure out exactly what you meant."

The Visionary smiled, "I wanted you to think," he said, "but I'm not sure I wanted you to lose any sleep. What I meant to communicate was that most organizations don't need to stop doing the things they are doing and set out on a new agenda. Most are already doing what needs to be done, they simply don't take advantage of the things they are *already* doing. I've often told organizations not to stop what they are doing, just turn every activity into a meaningful event to build relationships."

". . . Turn every activity into a meaningful relationship-building event."

"That's a curious thought," said the Frustrated Man. "During the week I examined my calendar and the calendar of my organization. I looked at all the events we had planned and asked myself the question, 'How can this be turned into something meaningful?'"

"That is precisely the right question to be asking," the Visionary responded. "Take, for example, a scheduled program. Some organizations have special programs planned throughout the year, every year. Why not turn those activities into events?"

"But how could you do that?" the Frustrated Man asked.

The Visionary leaned over as if to tell a secret. "Easily," he said. "Why not invite some of your category 'C' prospects to a special reception before a particular event and give them the opportunity to see your facility and meet some of your category 'A' patrons. After the program you could host another reception for another group. After all," he added, "punch and cookies don't cost that much and the relationship-building opportunities are extraordinary."

"Well, after our meeting last week, I was wondering how I could get people to attend events or involve them.

This might be a way. Right?" asked the Frustrated Man. "Absolutely," the Visionary agreed. "You could get 'C' prospects to attend and invite some of your 'B' and 'A' prospects to assist you. You've accomplished something in building relationships with each group and, more importantly, you have turned a regularly scheduled activity into a very significant relationship-building event."

"Do you have any other ideas?" the Frustrated Man asked.

"Many," the Visionary responded. "You have lunch everyday. Why not invite some of the key influencers in your community to join you. Rather than go to the neighborhood restaurant, why not invite them into your office for a catered lunch?"

"My office," the Frustrated Man said, "You've got to be kidding. We're so crowded at my organization, I hardly have a place to lay down my hat."

"All the better," said the Visionary. "What better way to communicate a need appropriately than to let someone see it. Once they see the circumstances under which you work to complete your very worthwhile service, they might be more inclined to support you."

"That makes sense," the Frustrated Man nodded. "Anything else?"

"Be careful now," the Visionary cautioned. "What will make your relationship-building program work is not necessarily my ideas. Your program is limited only by *your* creativity. You've already begun doing the right things; you're searching your calendar, evaluating your personal agenda, and asking the right questions. Don't stop, the answers are there."

"Well," the Frustrated Man smiled. "I was hoping you would make it easier for me. After all, if I can figure a way of getting out of some work, I'm not beyond trying!"

"I understand," the Visionary agreed, "but the real value of what you are learning now is that this is a *model*. It's a model you can build on and create *your* program around. If you understand the philosophy of the model and build upon it you will be successful. But if you follow someone else's program, you will never have ownership of what you truly must own to be successful."

"If you understand the philosophy of the model and build upon it you will be successful in building relationships."

The Frustrated Man responded, "I know you're right." He continued, "Can we review the steps in the model that we've covered until now?"

"Good idea," the Visionary nodded. "The first step in the process is to identify your prospects, those groups of individuals with whom you could build relationships. Remember, the numbers are almost infinite since you impact multiplied thousands either directly or indirectly."

"But," the Frustrated Man interjected, "a prospect really isn't a prospect to me until I have his name permanently recorded somewhere. Right?"

"Right," the Visionary agreed. "The second step in the model is to qualify your prospects. You can qualify them in a variety of ways. You might choose to do it by acknowledging the relationship they already have with you: nuclear, affinity or fringe. You might qualify them on the basis of what they can give, how they can assist you, or on the basis of their influence with others."

The Visionary continued, "the third step is cultivation. We've spent a lot of time here and for good reason. To the extent we are successful in cultivation, everything else falls into place. We talked about the transition that must occur from an emotional relationship to a rational one. Only rational relationships are sustainable and the goal of what we are doing is to establish sustainable, long term relationships with people. We've discussed how to track a developing relationship along with some ideas on the things we can do to facilitate these objectives."

"I guess we've covered a lot," the Frustrated Man said. "What's next?"

"The fourth step," the Visionary exclaimed, "I call the solicitation of our prospects."

Take Ten . . .

Take just ten minutes to evaluate how you might turn your organization's activities into meaningful developmental events.

1. Calendar Review. Review your calendar of activities for this year and make a list of those things you are currently doing that you might turn into a meaningful developmental event.

2. List Opportunities. Alongside each of those you have listed above, indicate what you could do to turn that activity into an event.

Chapter Ten: Projects and Programs

W hen the Frustrated Man arrived the next week, he was directed into the office of the Visionary. The Visionary was sitting at the large roll-top desk completing some paper work.

"Come here," he said, motioning the Frustrated Man to the desk. "Do you know why people like roll-top desks?" he asked.

"Not really," the Frustrated Man responded, "I guess just because they like them."

"You're right about that," the Visionary agreed. "But most people like roll-top desks because they like cubby holes. Look at me, for example." He motioned with a wave of his hand to all the little drawers and cubby holes that were a part of his desk. "I like to put the home mortgage payment book in here, and I have this little drawer over here where I can put all my receipts for income tax purposes."

The Visionary was obviously excited about his desk. He stood up and began to walk over to the fireplace. "I wanted you to see that," he began, "because there is a very important lesson there. Always remember, people like cubby holes."

"Always remember, people like cubby holes."

"Well, I know this might sound strange to you," smiled the Frustrated Man, "but I'm not sure I see where you are going."

The Visionary slapped his knees and began to laugh. "Well," he continued, "let me explain. Today I want to talk to you about asking people to support your organization. It's the fourth step in the relationship-building model; it's called solicitation. There are a variety of ways that you might ask for that support, but the most effective way is to seek the involvement of people in conjunction with an established program. You see, a program is a cubby hole."

"Sorry," the Frustrated Man said, nodding his head, "I still don't see it."

"Well, let's say that I was a businessman and you were asking me to give $25 to your organization. Would you be more likely to respond to me if I just stopped by to ask you for $25 or if I invited you to become a member of your Corporate Partnership Program, participation in which is granted to those businessmen who contribute $25?"

"I guess the Corporate Partnership Program would be more appealing," the Frustrated Man responded.

"You're right," agreed the Visionary. "And the reason is because your Corporate Partnership Program is a cubby hole. People like cubby holes!" The Visionary leaned back, feeling triumphant in the fact that he had proved his point.

"Oh, I see," said the Frustrated Man. "A program is more likely to be responded to than a straight out appeal."

"Generally speaking, yes," said the Visionary. "Programs provide people something they can plug into. And they don't have to be fund-raising in their orientation. People would rather be on a committee or task force than just to be asked for advice. They would prefer sponsoring a child to being admonished to encourage one.

And they would more likely participate in a Leadership Circle than lend their support singularly to a particular cause."

"Programs provide people something they can plug into."

"Then, I should think about various programs when I seek to engage the support of people for my organization?"

"Yes," agreed the Visionary. "But there is something else that is very important. It's called the Rule of Communication. It's a rule you should consider whenever you ask anyone for anything."

The Frustrated Man reached for his note pad. "The Rule of Communication." He asked, "What is that?"

"The Rule of Communication is almost as important as the Rule of Linkage. Simply stated the rule is this: one on one is best; the further you remove yourself from the ideal, the less likely it is that you'll get the response you want." The Visionary leaned over to make certain the Frustrated Man had written the definition exactly.

He continued, "If you want someone to support you, the best way to gain that support is to go to them personally and ask. The further you remove yourself from that ideal, the less likely it is that they will support you. Imagine," he went on, "asking twenty people in a group to support your organization. Some of them are getting the message and others are praying that some of them will get the message!"

The Frustrated Man laughed. "That would be true of a lot of people I know. They would be praying that the guy at the end of the table would get the message, because he has lots of money!"

"Exactly," smiled the Visionary, "so the best way is always the direct way. But that's not always possible, given the fact that we are dealing with hundreds, even thousands of people. So sometimes we have to resort to other means, things like calling on the telephone or sending letters."

"Is one of those mediums better than the other?" asked the Frustrated Man.

"Well, what do you think?" the Visionary asked, turning the tables.

"If you want someone to support you, the best way to gain that support is to go to them personally and ask."

"I guess the phone would be better than a letter; at least it is direct?" he answered questioningly.

"You're right," the Visionary agreed, "but there is no substitute for one on one."

"Now, let me see," the Frustrated Man said, pondering. "The best way to ask people to become involved in my organization is to go directly to them. And the best way to secure their involvement is through a program, right?"

"Right," smiled the Visionary.

"Well, earlier in our visits you talked about projects," the Frustrated Man continued. "What's the difference between a project and a program?"

"That's a great question." The Visionary reached for a pen and paper. "A project is anything that you do that tends to elicit an emotional response. A program tends to elicit a rational response. What you are striving for is the sustained involvement of your constituents and that will only occur as they rationally understand and support your mission."

"A project . . . tends to elicit an
emotional response.
A program tends to elicit a rational response."

The Frustrated Man responded, "I understand what a program is, but remind me again about projects."

"Well, a project would be something like a fund-raiser. Sometimes organizations will have pie sales or raffles. And when people respond to them," the Visionary explained, "they are generally responding emotionally to someone or something. Maybe they just are hungry and want a piece of pie!"

"I can relate to that," laughed the Frustrated Man. "There's an organization in our town that sells smoked chicken. A lot of charitable groups engage them to help them raise funds. I think I have supported just about everything under the sun, just to get a piece of chicken!"

"You probably did," the Visionary agreed, "and there is little likelihood that you will support any of those charitable groups in an ongoing way because it wasn't a rational understanding of their mission that prompted you to buy the chicken."

The Frustrated Man responded, "Well, you're right again. But," he continued, "is there any value in projects at all?"

"Oh yes," said the Visionary, "projects used to facilitate relational goals are great. Too often, however, we look at projects as an end in themselves. We take the money we earn in a fund-raiser and race to the bank. We expend a lot of energy to make it happen but it doesn't take us anywhere."

"Projects should always be used to facilitate relational goals."

"Can we talk more about that?" asked the Frustrated Man. "I'm afraid I have a lot of worn out constituents who haven't been getting much mileage out of the things they have done. I'd like to help them."

"All right," said the Visionary, "let's begin."

Take Ten . . .

Take just ten minutes to list the projects and programs in which your organization is currently involved. Then take time to think through the kinds of activities you might consider as you move into the future.

1. Project List. Create a list of all the projects with which you are currently involved.

2. Program List. Create a list of all the programs with which you are currently involved.

3. Idea List. What kinds of projects or programs could enhance the fulfillment of your organization's mission?

Chapter Eleven: Setting Short Term Goals

The idea that projects could be used to facilitate relationship-building goals was a brand new thought for the Frustrated Man. The Visionary had explained that projects should never be thought of as an end in themselves but always a means to accomplish a worthy end.

Projects take a great deal of time and energy. People in his organization were getting tired and didn't respond very positively to new project ideas. It seemed that everyone knew there must be a better way but no one had discovered it yet. The Visionary, however, seemed to have an answer.

"What we must do is to define what must be accomplished every year, every step, if we are to reach the top."

The Visionary began, almost pondering. "You know," he said, "I've often told organizations that if they could tell me where they wanted to go, what it would cost, and when they wanted to be there, that I could tell them how to get there, provided that I had a clear picture of where they were."

"What do you mean?" asked the Frustrated Man, "how to get there?"

The Visionary responded, "Look at every year as a step on a staircase. The staircase leads us to where we are going. What we must do is to define what must be accomplished every year, every step, if we are to get to the top."

"And that can be done?" the Frustrated Man asked hopefully.

"Oh, yes," the Visionary agreed. "And with a great deal of specificity. You see, there are established benchmarks that every organization should seek to achieve. For instance you should set goals for the number of people you have on your database, the number of people that are supporting you financially, the size of the average gift you receive, things like that."

"You could go even further," he continued. "You need to know how many prospects you have in each category. You see, it's not just numbers that will determine your success, it is the quality of the numbers that you have on your database."

"I'm beginning to understand that," the Frustrated Man responded, "but how are all these goals accomplished?"

"Through projects and programs. Everything we do kind of revolves around all the issues we've already talked about. You see," the Visionary continued, "that's what I meant when I said projects should be used as relationship-building facilitators. Some projects are an excellent way to add qualified names to your database, and many can be great entry level opportunities to bring people out of the sea of prospects onto your front porch. It is unfortunate that most organizations miss the real value of projects. If the project is a fund-raiser, what is raised should only be incidental to other, more important things."

"Like getting names or providing the entry level opportunity?" asked the Frustrated Man.

"Exactly," agreed the Visionary. But it's not just the names that are important. It is how many names and the kind of names that are important. Every project should have quantifiable goals. Things like, 'we want to add this many names to our database.' Or 'we want to add this many nuclear names, or this many affinity names, or this many fringe names.'"

"Every project should have quantifiable goals."

"You mean you can do that?" the Frustrated Man asked surprisingly.

"Of course," said the Visionary. "In fact, setting quantifiable goals will add dimension to your project and a great deal of focus to your planning. After all," he continued, "if you want to add fringe names, you're not going to solicit the involvement of nuclear prospects."

The Frustrated Man thought quietly. "So," he said, "There is some value in projects?"

"Oh yes, yes indeed," the Visionary exclaimed. "Projects can be of great value if they help you to get where you want to go. Every relationship-building program should consider projects to accomplish what projects are good at accomplishing. But the main emphasis of every organization's developmental focus should be primarily on programs."

"Because they generate rational support?" asked the Frustrated Man.

"Exactly and . . . "

". . . because it's only rational support that is sustainable," laughed the Frustrated Man.

"You're certainly catching on," smiled the Visionary. "Rational support is important for many reasons. When we come back next week, I would like to explain the most important reason of all why it is so essential that your organization pursue the rational support of its constituents."

"I can hardly wait," the Frustrated Man winked.

Take Ten . . .

Take just ten minutes to assess your short term goals.

1. List the Areas. Short term goals invariably fall into various categories. List all the areas where you must make progress in your organization this year.

2. Be Specific. Alongside each area listed above, be as specific as you can in determining what your precise goal for the current year should be.

Chapter Twelve: Determining Your Potential

Since their very first meeting, the Visionary had emphasized over and over again the importance of an organization engaging the support of others in a rational way. He reminded the Frustrated Man frequently that only rationally committed people sustain their support and, in fact, he had gone one step further to define success as the ability of an organization to sustain the support of its constituents.

Now the Visionary had implied that there were other very important reasons why an organization should pursue the rational involvement of others. It was with that thought in mind that the Frustrated Man came to his meeting with the Visionary.

After sitting down near the fireplace, the Visionary began to speak. "I've had the opportunity of counseling thousands of organizations just like yours. I've met some very wonderful people, people much like yourself. These people are involved in their respective enterprises because they strongly believe that the existence of the organizations they represent contributes to the health of their communities, indeed the very health of the society of which we are a part."

The Frustrated Man was listening intently. He deeply respected the Visionary Man for not only was he very knowledgeable about what organizations needed to do, but he also seemed to be driven with a passion to help others. He had never felt that he was imposing on the Visionary, despite the fact that they met regularly week after week. The Visionary had not ever asked about reimbursement; he seemed to be genuinely interested in trying to help.

"One thing that I have seen," the Visionary continued, "is that most people who sit in the same seat that you do in their respective organizations have a vision for their work that is far greater than their ability to pay for it."

"most people . . . have a vision for their work that is far greater than their ability to pay for it."

The Frustrated Man seemed almost to jump to attention. "My," he agreed, "I can't begin to tell you how many times I have been told that my head is in the clouds. My board often acts preoccupied when I share with them these dreams, almost acting like they really wish I would just keep quiet."

"And how does that make you feel?" asked the Visionary.

The Frustrated Man paused, thinking. Then he spoke carefully, "At first it made me feel that I wasn't really communicating well, so I would think of other ways to share my dreams. Sometimes I would bring charts and graphs to validate a point. Once in a while my presentation would almost demand a response, but nothing would ever go anywhere. Eventually, after months, if not years of hitting my head against the wall, I've finally developed an almost apathetic attitude. Frankly," he continued, "if they don't seem to care, why should I?"

There was a sense of deep resignation that seemed to characterize the Frustrated Man. It was something that the Visionary had seen many times before. The Visionary was obviously concerned; a look of pathos crossed his face.

It was the Visionary's turn to pause and think. He was obviously measuring his words and when he spoke, he did so with passion. "You have very clearly articulated the problem. But it doesn't have to be, and that's the thing that causes me so much frustration in my work. There is absolutely no reason why any organization should not be able to fulfill its dreams. Can you imagine," he spoke with more fervor now, "the differences that we might see in our society if organizations like yours really succeeded?"

"Every organization has . . . developmental

potential. It's the amount of money that they

could raise to fund a capital need."

"Oh, of course," agreed the Frustrated Man, "but society doesn't seem to care, so why should anyone else?"

"But we must work to make society care," the Visionary pleaded, "and that's why all the things we have talked about up to this point are so absolutely essential for every organization to pursue aggressively. That's the beginning, but do you know why that is the beginning?"

"Sounds to me like a set up question," the Frustrated Man answered.

"Yes, I guess it is," the Visionary said. It seemed that his friend was catching on to his ways. "Well then, let me answer the question," the Visionary smiled. "Every organization has what I call developmental potential. Developmental potential is a number. It's the amount of money that any organization could raise if it had to fund a capital need. It's a number that is calculable, and it is one number that every organization like yours in this country really must know."

"Slow down," the Frustrated Man said. He was writing feverishly on the pad in front of him and needed a few minutes of breathing time. "What you're saying," he began, "is that if I needed to raise money for a particular project, say a new building, it is possible to determine now what I could raise?"

"Exactly," the Visionary nodded. "I will share with you a formula that will enable you to know today how much you could raise if you were to try to raise money for that new building."

"Well," the Frustrated Man continued, "I guess I'm all ears."

"Every organization like yours is already doing things to raise money to fund your ongoing needs. That money is coming to you in a variety of ways. You are involved in some projects and you are involved in some fund-raising programs." The Visionary paused.

Filling in the vacant time, the Frustrated Man chimed in, "And, some of that money is more valuable to our long term needs." He paused for a second and then added, "Let me guess; the money that we raised in our projects is not nearly as valuable to us as what we raised through our programs, right?"

"You've learned that lesson very well," the Visionary responded. "But let me tell you why. Only rational income is sustainable on an ongoing basis and it is the average of your annual rational income that will determine your developmental potential."

"You mean," the Frustrated Man asked, "what I should do is take an average of all my rational giving for the last two or three years?"

"Right," agreed the Visionary. "Rational giving is what I call real support. It is the only support that you raise on an annual basis that is sustainable because it was given for the right reasons. People chose to support you for rational reasons, because they understand your mission and have chosen to 'buy into' that mission in a practical way."

"Then," the Frustrated Man responded, "what I need to do is look at all of the income I received and average out what I can determine came from people who rationally gave as opposed to those who may have given for emotional reasons?"

"That's right. And once you have that average," he added, "multiply that number times five. What you will have is the base point for determining your organization's development potential."

The base point for determining developmental potential is the amount of "real" support your organization receives each year.

"Why am I using a multiplier of five?" asked the Frustrated Man.

"Because," explained the Visionary, "there is a rule in fund-raising that goes something like this. The average donor to a discretionary gifting cause is capable of giving five to ten times his average annual gift if properly motivated in a capital funding campaign."

"Slow down," the Frustrated Man urged. He was writing as fast as he could on the pad in front of him. "What do you mean by a 'discretionary gifting cause?'"

"That can be a bit confusing, can't it?" the Visionary exclaimed. "I suppose, technically speaking, all giving is discretionary. After all, we don't have to give. But some people make distinctions in their giving. Those that give regularly to their churches, for instance, give for different reasons than they do if they also give to your organization."

"Oh," the Frustrated Man nodded, "I understand now. My wife and I give to our church but we have developed a formula that determines how much those gifts will be. It's a percentage of our income. But we also give to other causes. We give to the organization with which we work; we give to the United Way, to the local Boy Scouts, and the American Cancer Society."

"There you go," the Visionary said. "Let's call your church giving 'indiscretionary' and let's call all your other giving 'discretionary.' If you were giving to your church $10,000 each year, it's hardly likely that you could give five to ten times that amount if you were asked to support a new building campaign. But, if you were giving the American Cancer Society $100 every year and had been doing that faithfully over a long period of time, the likelihood is that you could make a campaign pledge of $500 or $1,000 if that pledge could be paid out over a two or three year period."

---

*"Your developmental potential is based on . . .
real giving. Project, or emotional giving, has
no bearing whatsoever on
developmental potential!"*

"That would be over and above what I am already doing?" the Frustrated Man asked. "You know, if they are like our organization, we can hardly do without that income."

"I understand," agreed the Visionary. "And you're right. Let's look at a five year period. During that five years you would give $100 a year to support ongoing needs and now you are being asked to give $500 to $1,000, in addition to that, to support a capital funding need. Over five years, in actuality, you have made gifts totaling $1,000-$1,500 instead of $500."

"I probably could do that," the Frustrated Man thought aloud. "It would be stretching it, but if they had a legitimate need, I probably could and would give to support their need."

"And that would be true of most people," said the Visionary. "But there is a very important point to be made here. Your developmental potential is based on what we are calling real giving. Project, or emotional giving, has no bearing whatsoever on developmental potential."

The Frustrated Man thought for a moment and then asked, "So an organization that funds its short term needs on a series of funding projects and has done that consistently over a period of many years is not really very healthy developmentally, is it?"

The Visionary looked very satisfied. "You are absolutely right. And that is why we must change the way we are doing things in organizations like yours. You can not afford to spend time 'treading water' just to stay alive. You must begin building now for tomorrow and the only way you can do that is by building your annual levels of real support. Year after year."

"I'm afraid we have done very little in my organization to posture ourselves for the future. In fact," he continued, "this whole conversation is a bit disconcerting. We've spent too many years trying to stay alive and relatively few, if any, building for the future."

"You and hundreds, if not thousands of other organizations," said the Visionary. "Many groups, like yours, that have been around for many years are facing the risk of closure today and that would be a great loss to our society. Probably the reason why your board seems so apathetic to you when you share your dreams is because they feel that there is absolutely no hope whatsoever that you would be able to fund them."

"I'm beginning to understand," the Frustrated Man said solemnly. "Does all of this that we are talking about impact my long range planning?"

"Absolutely," said the Visionary. "In fact many organizations build their long range or strategic plan around an understanding of this concept. Maybe next week I can show you how."

At that point the Visionary stood up, signaling an end to this week's meeting.

Take Ten . . .

Take just ten minutes to calculate your organization's developmental potential.

1. Developmental Potential. What is the developmental potential of your organization? (Calculate developmental potential by multiplying your average annual real support by five).

2. Your Needs. If you were to calculate the cost of funding the vision of your organization, how much would it be?

3. Timing. When do you need to achieve your vision (by what year)?

Chapter Thirteen: Planning Your Future

The previous meeting had motivated the Frustrated Man to return to his office and analyze gifting patterns. Each year his organization was required to raise a great deal of money to support the services it provided. Some of those funds came from fund-raising projects, and there was also a small group of people who chose to give to the organization each year.

As he began to total numbers, he quickly realized that his organization was poorly postured to fund the great vision he had for the future. He had allowed himself to dream again about that future. As he mentally began to calculate what that vision might cost he realized that the price of his vision might be nearly a million dollars. As he calculated his developmental potential, recognizing that he was receiving each year about $20,000 in real support, he came up with a figure of just under $100,000.

That realization caused him to think carefully. Part of him was terribly frustrated as he reflected on wasted years—so much energy expended to stay alive, energy that for all practical purposes took the organization nowhere. Another part of him, however, was filled with renewed hope. He knew that his dreams could be realized. There was hope, a great deal of hope, that his organization could achieve its potential.

When the Frustrated Man arrived the morning of their next meeting, he was greeted enthusiastically by the Visionary.

"Well, tell me, my friend," he began, "What have you been doing this week?"

The Frustrated Man smiled. He had a pretty good idea that the Visionary knew exactly what he had been doing. "Well," he began, "I started looking at some numbers, and I've determined that we are quite a distance from being able to achieve some of the goals I have for this organization."

"At least you know," commented the Visionary, "and there is something to be said for that. Most organizations don't have the foggiest idea about where they are, and when asked how they are going to get to where they want to go, they look like you've just asked them to explain the law of relativity."

"Yes," the Frustrated Man agreed, "long range planning in our organization is pretty short term! We figure if we can survive another year, we've made real progress!"

"Just about every organization I have ever worked with," the Visionary explained, "was in the same boat. So look at it this way," he added, "now you are a good deal ahead of others in what you know."

"I suppose that was intended to give me some comfort," the Frustrated Man smiled, "but I'm still a long way from where I want to be."

"But you have a solid foundation on which you can build," the Visionary added, "and that's what we should focus on."

The Frustrated Man shared the results of his week's work. As he concluded his presentation, he added, "I'm really quite a way off from being able to achieve my vision for this organization. And according to your formula, in order for me to have a potential to raise a million dollars, I would need to have an average annual real support base of $200,000. I really don't see that as being too likely in the near future."

"That's true with many organizations," the Visionary

agreed. "So, as organizations plan for the future, many of them do their planning in phases. There are many good reasons to consider a capital campaign. First of all, most will probably never have the disposable resources available to them to fund major expansion. Secondly, when an organization successfully completes a capital campaign, annual gift income will generally increase. Often as much as 30%."

". . . Many organizations plan for their
future in phases."

"But," the Frustrated Man interrupted, "I've known some organizations that have had a capital funding campaign and they haven't achieved their goal. Rather than being a positive experience, it ended up being disastrous."

"That can happen," the Visionary explained. "Often goals are set unrealistically high with no consideration whatever to what has historically been happening in the organization. So they enter a campaign to raise a million dollars and end up raising $100,000. Now that $100,000," the Visionary added, "may be more than that organization has ever raised in its history, but what people will remember is that they were $900,000 short of their goal."

The Frustrated Man added, "And that has a public relational impact that may take years to overcome."

"Precisely," the Visionary said with authority. "And that is why you must plan prudently, always with one eye on what is realistic for now."

The Visionary leaned back in his chair and began to speak. "There is a rule relating to capital campaigns that is important to remember. The rule is that you should not begin a new capital campaign until five years after the beginning of the previous one. If you began a campaign in 2000, you should not begin another until 2005. The rule is based on another rule and that is that a developmental generation is five years."

"There you go again," the Frustrated Man smiled. "Slow down now. I can understand what you are saying about not beginning a capital campaign within five years of the beginning of the previous one, but what's this business about a developmental generation."

". . . Plan prudently, always with one eye on what is realistic for now."

"Well if an organization does developmental work consistently, year after year," the Visionary explained, "every five years there will be enough change in your constituency to justify a new campaign. You see," he added, "you are always building on what you have done in the past."

"But what bearing does all of this have on planning?" the Frustrated Man asked.

"Well, according to your calculations," the Visionary responded, "you have a current development potential of about $100,000. My guess is that you could probably begin the funding of your vision for the future if you had $100,000 at your disposal."

"You bet I could," the Frustrated Man interjected.

"Well, some organizations choose to move into a capital funding campaign to fund an early phase of the long range plan. After the campaign is over and people have paid their pledges to you, as I already inferred, giving tends to go up. And, as real support increases annually, so does your developmental potential."

"So in five years I could do another campaign," the Frustrated Man added, "and it is likely that I could raise more than in the first one; and then I might be able to fund a second phase of my vision. Is that right?"

"There you go again," the Visionary laughed. "And you're right. It may be practically impossible for you ever to bring your real support to high enough levels to fund your vision through one capital campaign. In that case you should phase in your plan for the future. Eventually you will get there."

"It may be practically impossible for you ever to bring your real support to high enough levels to fund your vision through one capital campaign. In that case you should phase in your plan for the future."

"That's incredible," the Frustrated Man mused. "I really can see the possibility of my vision being accomplished. But, it will take some pro-active planning."

"What a great word," the Visionary responded. "There are two ways to lead any organization, pro-actively or re-actively; but it is only those organizations that pro-actively plan that generally sustain their impact into the future."

The Visionary stood up and began to speak as they walked to the door. There is still another step in the relationship-building process that we need to talk about, I call it 'Sustaining our Constituents.' Let's make that the focus of our next visit."

Take Ten . . .

Take just ten minutes to think about your future.

1. Goals. Make a list of the goals you would like to achieve in the next five years.

2. Cost. What do you feel it would cost for you to achieve these goals?

3. Phasing. Can you think of ways in which these goals can be phased in over a period of time? Write down your ideas.

Chapter Fourteen: Sustaining Your Constituents

The Visionary had explained in a previous meeting that most organizations look at the things they do as ends in themselves. If they conduct a particular activity, they look at that activity as something that occurs on a specific day. Once the activity has been completed and the day of the activity gone by, thoughts generally focus on the next thing they must do.

The thought of "turning every activity into a meaningful relationship-building event" changed the Frustrated Man's entire focus as it related to his work. He began to evaluate his schedule, to look at his own calendar as well as that of his organization and to conceive how he might leverage an event to gain from it the maximum potential.

These thoughts were running through his mind when he walked into the office of the Visionary. Immediately upon taking their seats in front of the fireplace, the Visionary began to speak.

"We've come a long way in our discussions. If your organization is to experience success in ways that you dream of, you must begin an orchestrated pro-active process of building relationships." He continued, "There are some very specific things that you must do. You need to identify those with whom you could build a relationship, qualify those people as it relates to your needs and their potential, cultivate them, and eventually come to a point where you provide them an opportunity to share in your work."

"That's the solicitation process, right?" asked the

Frustrated Man.

"Yes," the Visionary continued. "But don't think of solicitation as simply what we do to engage the financial support of our constituents. People have so much to give besides money, and they can assist your developing organization in so many ways. But your constituents deserve the courtesy of being asked. You shouldn't just assume that people will help, and you mustn't presume upon people. You need to work to build a relationship with them and ask them for their help when the need is there and the time is appropriate."

The Frustrated Man thought for a moment. "You know," he added, "I really don't like it when people simply *expect* me to do something. They don't bother to ask, or if they do, it is almost as if I don't have a choice."

"Most everyone feels like that," the Visionary agreed. "But there is another side to that story too. Once," he continued, "I asked someone to support financially an organization I represented. They gave a very large gift and were thrilled to do it. When I asked them why they had never done this before they said . . . "

". . . because I was never asked," the Frustrated Man interrupted.

"You're right," smiled the Visionary. "So we really must not ignore the solicitation step in this process." The Visionary stopped a few seconds and then began again, "There is one more step that you must remember, and that is the procedure you follow to sustain the support of your constituents."

"I know that is the goal of this process," the Frustrated Man interjected, "but you are also making it a precise step?" He looked confused.

"That's right," the Visionary continued. "You see, too often someone does something for us and we accept their generosity and just go on without even acknowledging it. It's almost like we expect it and take no notice of what they did or what motivated them to do it."

" . . . too often, someone does something for us and we accept their generosity and go on."

"You mean," the Frustrated Man questioned, "we don't say thank you?"

"That certainly is part of it," the Visionary agreed, "but only part of it. People need to be thanked, they need to be acknowledged in appropriate ways for the contributions they make to your success. You have needed them to accomplish your objectives and *you will continue to need their active involvement* as you build for the future."

The Frustrated Man felt caught again, "Oops," he said, "I guess we don't always remember that it is people who got us to where we are and it will be people who will get us to where we want be."

"You've hit it," the Visionary smiled. "And once organizations remember that, they will be well on their way to success. And there's another thing," he added. "You need to remember that people give to people. They don't give to buildings or necessarily to programs; they give to those people whose lives will be enriched by those buildings or those programs."

"That's rather a profound thought," the Frustrated Man mused. "It sounds to me that we need to emphasize people more."

"You would be very wise to do that," the Visionary agreed. "You see, if you are to sustain the involvement of people, you must acknowledge their current involvement. You must thank them well and you can't simply drop them; you must continue to cultivate them and seek meaningful ways to engage them in your developing needs."

The Frustrated Man was writing notes on what was being said. He looked up curiously and asked, "Can you help me think of some ways that I could acknowledge people? I mean, how do you really thank people for the things they do to help you?"

". . . people give to people. They don't give to buildings or necessarily to programs, they give to those people whose lives will be enriched by those buildings and programs."

The Visionary thought and said, "Well, you could begin by *saying* thank you," he began. "But there is a variety of other ways. Certainly a letter of appreciation is appropriate, and some organizations will give plaques to acknowledge the involvement of constituents. I've attended hundreds of Appreciation Dinners, special events intended to gather together all those who have provided assistance to an organization within a given period of time."

The Visionary continued, "I know one school that asks each of their students to sponsor a donor. They stay in regular communication with that individual during the year, sending them cards and expressing thanks to them for making it possible for the students to receive an education at that school."

"That's a neat idea," the Frustrated Man said. "Sure makes it pretty personal."

"You're right about that." The Visionary shared more ideas, "Other organizations have an annual phone-athon, not for the purpose of asking but for the purpose of thanking."

"I like that," interjected the Frustrated Man, "and if the people making the phone calls are the ones who are benefitting from the services you provide, that would make it even more meaningful."

The Visionary continued to be very impressed with the Frustrated Man. He was pleased when he saw the ways he grasped concepts and applied them to his organization.

"Sustaining the involvement of people," the Visionary added, "is key to your long term success. You want your supporters to continue to support you, and what you do after they become involved will pretty much determine if they will continue to help."

"Sustaining the involvement of people . . .
is key to your long term success."

The Visionary thought for a moment and then added, "You know, one night I went to an appreciation dinner for an organization. They were expressing thanks to their friends and wanted to acknowledge particularly one donor who had made a very substantial gift. As I remember it," he recalled, "this lady had given money to help support a program for nurses. At an appropriate time in the program, nearly 70 nurses who had benefitted already from things she had done came forward and handed her a long stemmed red rose."

"Wow," interjected the Frustrated Man, "that had to be pretty moving."

"Oh it was," agreed the Visionary, "there was hardly a dry eye in the place. But, more importantly, the lady felt like the most appreciated woman in the room, if not the world. And guess what?" he asked.

"What?" responded the Frustrated Man.

"That lady," he answered, "continues to support that organization. Generously, year after year. You see, she felt appreciated for what she had done, and she has sustained her involvement."

There was a long pause and then the Visionary stood, "Well, that about does it. You've got a model with five steps: Identification, Qualification, Cultivation, Solicitation, and Sustaining. Now all you need to do is apply the principles and maybe, just maybe, you'll see some very positive changes in the way you personally do things. You might also see some very positive differences in your organization."

"I have already," the Frustrated Man responded. "But before you send me off to make it on my own, could you help me in defining what it is that I can do now?"

"Certainly," agreed the Visionary. "Let's meet again next week and see if we can bring this all to some kind of conclusion."

Take Ten . . .

Take just ten minutes to reflect on how you demonstrate to people your appreciation of their involvement with your organization.

1. Evaluation of Thanks. Make a list of the ways your organization expresses appreciation to people.

2. Ideas. What kinds of things could your organization do to express thanks to people more effectively?

Chapter Fifteen:
Defining Success

For several weeks now the Frustrated Man had met with the Visionary. During their time together, his vision for the organization with which he worked had been rekindled.

It wasn't as if the fires had gone out. The Frustrated Man had always felt a special passion for the work to which he had committed his life. The organization he represented provided him an avenue to help others. And others had been helped. It was just that there were so many more that needed the services his agency was equipped to provide. In order to meet these needs, it was essential to have the resources. And therein lay the problem.

Every time the Frustrated Man shared his ideas, his vision for the future, it was met with resistance. It wasn't the kind of bitter antagonism that sometimes characterizes opposition, it was resistance borne more out of apathy and indifference.

But there is only so much resistance, no matter how it presents itself, that anyone can endure without its making an impact. And the impact that it had upon the frustrated man was hopelessness. He had resigned himself merely to continue plodding along. He had also pretty much given up thinking that his dreams could ever be achieved.

His introduction to the Visionary Man was almost accidental. A friend passed him a business card which led to a meeting which led to a relationship which led to more meetings which eventually led to a change in outlook. That change in outlook not only changed his attitude but his organization, as well.

As he arrived at the office of the Visionary on this day, he realized they were close to the end of their regular meetings. But there were just a few things remaining that he had to resolve.

As they took their seats, the Frustrated man began, "I really am grateful that you would give me more time. Our meetings have been very helpful, and already I have put in place some changes within my organization. I'm beginning to see a change in those with whom I work, even among members of my Board of Directors."

"Well, that is something in itself," the Visionary exclaimed, "for once your board captures a vision, that makes your job a whole lot easier."

"I agree," nodded the Frustrated man, "but that's the problem. How do I keep them excited, keep them focused on the future?"

" . . . once your board captures a vision, that
makes your job a whole lot easier."

"By letting them experience success," the Visionary responded. "But success is often a relative thing. At the end of the year someone may ask whether or not our organization was successful that year. Usually," he continued, "someone will state that they feel you were very successful. They will refer to a particular event or two and point out what had been accomplished. Inevitably someone else will suggest that perhaps you weren't that successful after all. They'll look at figures and suggest that they don't justify optimism, or they'll interpret a particular event in an entirely different way. If you have ten people evaluating success, you are very likely to have ten different opinions."

"And that's my point," said the Frustrated Man. "We have some momentum now and I hate to see us divided on something as crucial as our definition of success."

"Then define it," said the Visionary. "Define success in the kinds of quantifiable terms that everyone can relate to. Set an agenda, discuss it, and agree that this is a good agenda for the future. Make certain that the agenda can be quantifiably assessed; and at the end of the year, assess it. The key is objectivity."

"Define success in the kinds of quantifiable
terms that everyone can relate to . . .
the key is objectivity."

"I'm not sure I understand," the Frustrated Man responded, looking confused.

"Well, let's say that this year we want to increase our developmental potential by $50,000. That means we must increase our annual rational support by $10,000. That's pretty specific, isn't it?"

"Yes," the Frustrated man responded hesitantly.

"Don't look so confused," the Visionary smiled. "Either you make it or you don't. If you don't reach that goal, you might discuss why you didn't or what you could have done differently. But at least when you discuss success, as it relates to that issue, there is no confusion."

The Frustrated Man jotted down something on the pad in his lap. Then he said, "What other factors could you use to evaluate success?"

"Remember," he said, "when I suggested that you think of your goals in terms of a stairway and suggested to you that you should define the steps in quantifiable terms?"

The Frustrated Man nodded.

"Well, that's what I meant," the Visionary explained. "You need to define each step specifically. If a step represents one year, then you should seek to define what you want to accomplish in that year. It may include the amount of money you want to raise, how much of that money should come to you in the form of rational giving, how many donors you want to engage, how many people you want to add to your database, into what categories you want them to fall, the percentage of entry level participants you would like to convert . . . "

". . . whoa," interrupted the Frustrated Man, "slow down." He wrote furiously on the paper in front of him.

". . . the goals you set for this year need to bring you closer to where you want to be. You're building, always building."

"Sorry," the Visionary smiled, "I didn't mean to get quite so consumed. But remember, the goals you set for this year need to bring you closer to where you want to be. You're building, always building. And when your Board of Directors periodically evaluates your progress, it is always in light of a measurable goal. The closer you come to achieving it, no matter where you might be at the time the evaluation takes place, you are still closer than when you began. People need to see progress. It's the lack of progress," he added, "that yields despair and apathy."

"I've got it!" the Frustrated Man exclaimed triumphantly. "And you know, I don't even know how to begin to thank you. Thank you for what you have taught me and thank you for rekindling my vision."

The Visionary looked content, "I can accept that. The fulfillment I enjoy is in the evident change I have seen in you, in your attitude and outlook. The final satisfaction will occur when I hear of the progress of your organization. That, to me, is the ultimate thank you."

They stood, shook hands and the Frustrated Man left.

Take Ten . . .

Take just ten minutes to define success for you and your organization.

1. Areas of Emphasis. What areas do you intend to emphasize in your developmental program this year? List them in the space below.

2. Goals. What goals do you have for each of these areas? Seek to determine if they are realistic, given the time and resources that you can commit to development. List the goals alongside each initiative listed above.

Conclusion

Once there was a very fulfilled man.

The man was involved in a very worthy work. That enterprise helped many men and women. There were a great many people who shared his vision for his work and chose to support the agency of the fulfilled man in a variety of very creative ways.

The work of the fulfilled man flourished and many people shared in the joy of its success.

The fulfilled man was also called a Visionary.

About the Author

About Gerald H. Twombly:

Gerald H. Twombly is the Founder and President of Development Marketing Associates, Inc., an international consulting firm specializing in assisting organizations in areas related to constituent development and marketing. Mr. Twombly holds degrees from Miami Christian University and Grace Theological Seminary. Prior to beginning his own consulting firm, Mr. Twombly served as Vice President for Advancement at Grace College and Seminary. During his four year tenure in that position, Grace received international recognition for excellence in its advancement initiatives. Mr. Twombly has written six books, serves on the board of directors of several organizations and speaks to thousands of people every year on subjects related to marketing and constituent development. In addition, his biography has been included in several listings including Who's Who in the World.

He and his wife Susan reside in Indianapolis, Indiana.

Development Marketing Associates

Phone toll-free: 1-866-DMA-FIRST

"Equipping Others to Serve Others for the Glory of God"

Development Marketing Associates (DMA) is committed to providing developmental support to a wide range of Christian ministries throughout the world. In addition to fundraising, DMA focuses on other areas of the development function including: recruitment, retention, public relations, database management, and long range (strategic) planning. Specific ministries of DMA are outlined here for your convenience.

The DMA Professional Development Certification Program

Since 1993, DMA has provided courses that lead to professional certification for individuals serving in the development profession. The program is oriented to Christian ministries and course content is based on Biblical principles. The unique "relationship model" pioneered by DMA is fully developed in this two-year course. Students are required to complete two one-week training sessions and fulfill a supervised internship with a qualified non-profit organization. Courses are offered throughout the year in various locations throughout the United States.

Graduates of the program receive one of three professional certification designations:

CDE. *The Certified Development Executive®* designation is reserved for those individuals serving in non-profit Christian ministries.
CDP. *The Certified Development Professional®* designation is reserved for those working in elementary and secondary Christian schools.
CCDE. *The Certified Collegiate Development Executive®* designation is reserved for those working in Christian colleges, universities, and graduate schools.
CCME. *The Certified Church Ministry Executive®* is reserved for those individuals serving in administrative areas in local churches.

For a complete catalog describing the certification program and dates and locations of training sessions please contact DMA.

Consulting Services

DMA has worked with over 3,000 Christian ministries in all 50 states of the United States, 5 provinces of Canada, and 13 other countries around the world. Since its beginning in 1985, The Lord has used this ministry in raising nearly half a billion dollars to further the cause of Christ. A team of professional consultants is available to serve your organization. The consulting services provided through DMA include the following:

- **Development Management.** DMA will provide overall supervision of the development program of your organization. This cost-effective program designed for small non-profits includes a DMA Associate working each month with the organization in addressing all "leading development indicators" and training a representative from the organization in *The DMA Professional Development Certification Program*.
- **Pre-Campaign Analysis Program.** DMA provides a vital service to organization's preparing for a major capital funding campaign in the Pre-Campaign Analysis. A team of DMA Associate Consultants come to your location and interview key constituents, guide in the administration of exclusive DMA assessment tools, identify prospective major donors and charitable foundations that might choose to fund your project, provide you with a dollar amount that represents what we believe you could raise should you move forward in your campaign, and provide you a complete timeline and recommended organizational structure for initiating a successful funding campaign.
- **Campaign Management.** DMA manages scores of campaigns for churches, schools, and colleges each year ranging in size from $1 million to $30 million.
- **Specialty Consulting.** On-site consulting sevices are available from DMA in other critical areas of non-profit management. Among them are consulting support in public relational imaging, student recruitment and retention, strategic planning, and development audits.

Development Newsletter and Website

Each month DMA sends to thousands of organizations a free Development Newsletter with poignant tips on ways organizations can improve their development program. This newsletter is mailed via e-mail to non-profit organizations throughout the world. Subscribers can download articles, sample letters, funding proposals, and other valuable resources. All information provided on the website is made available at no cost. To subscribe for your personal newsletter, register at our website: www.developmentmarketing.com.

Special Seminars and Conferences

DMA promotes several training seminars and special conferences for those involved in non-profit ministry. For more information about forthcoming programs and Jerry Twombly's speaking schedule, check out our website at: www.developmentmarketing.com.